CHRISTMAS PROGRAMS
for the
Church

Plays, Poems, and Ideas for All Ages

Carpenter's Son Publishing

Published by Carpenter's Son Publishing, Franklin, Tennessee.

Published in association with Larry Carpenter of Christian Book Services, LLC. www.christianbookservices.com

Cover and Interior Layout Design by Suzanne Lawing

Printed in the United States of America

978-1-942587-53-8

Contents

Kids

Youth

Adults

General

Kids

Cookie Theater

by Diana C. Derringer

SUMMARY: *A mother and children make cookies while learning about Christmas.*

CHARACTERS:
Mother: older girl or young woman
Tony: small boy
Tonya: small girl
Taylor: small girl or boy

SETTING: *a family kitchen*

PROPS: *table or counter top, cookie dough, Christmas cookie cutters, cookie sheet, plate of baked cookies, Bible*

COSTUMES: *contemporary clothing*

Children cut out cookies and place on the cookie sheet while Mother supervises. A plate of baked cookies sits to the side.

MOTHER: Hooray! Our last batch of cookies.

CHILDREN: Hooray!

TONY: Then we get to eat!

CHILDREN: Hooray!

MOTHER: Let's have a little fun with these cookies.

TAYLOR: Yeah, let's! How?

MOTHER: Okay. Here's the plan. Every time you cut out a cookie, I want you to tell us what your cookie is. Got that?

TONY: Sure. That's easy.

MOTHER: Then I want you to think of a Christmas song about it.

TONY: Got it.

MOTHER: Then I want you to think of something in the Bible about it.

TONYA: Whoa! That might be hard.

MOTHER: That's what makes it fun. You have to put on your thinking caps.

Mother and children make a twisting motion above their heads.

MOTHER: Taylor, you have a cookie ready to bake. Tell us what it is.

TAYLOR: Mine's a bell.

MOTHER: Can you think of a Christmas song about bells?

TAYLOR: You bet! "Jingle Bells!"

MOTHER: That works. Want to lead us?

Taylor leads group singing "Jingle Bells."

MOTHER: Now, Taylor, can you think of a Bible verse about bells?

Taylor and the other children frown as they think.

MOTHER: You know what? That's a really hard one. There are a few verses, like Exodus 28:34, that describe the robes of Old Testament priests. *(turns in Bible and reads)* Since this one's so hard, how about other musical instruments?

TAYLOR: I know! Didn't David play a harp?

MOTHER: I'm impressed, Taylor. He did indeed. Great job! *(high five)* Let's see, *(looks in Bible)* here's a verse that lists a bunch of instruments, including the harp. *(reads 1 Chronicles 13:8)* I also love Psalm 150:3–6. *(reads)* Okay, next?

TONY: I made an angel.

MOTHER: That you did, Tony. Can you think of an angel song?

TONY: How about "Angels We Have Heard on High"?

MOTHER: Oh, that's a beautiful song. Lead us in a verse.

All sing "Angels We Have Heard on High."

MOTHER: Now, how about an angel Bible verse?

TONY: Well, the angels told the shepherds when Jesus was born.

MOTHER: Good job, Tony. *(high five)* Do you know where we find that?

TONY: *(scratches head and wrinkles brow)* Luke 2 somewhere.

MOTHER: Right again. *(reads Luke 2:8–15)*

TAYLOR: Tony's was a lot easier than mine.

MOTHER: You're right, Taylor. His was a lot easier, but you still came up with something, didn't you?

TAYLOR: Yes, I did!

MOTHER: Your turn, Tonya.

TONYA: I have a Christmas tree, but I already know the Bible doesn't have Christmas trees in it. *(near tears)* That's not fair.

MOTHER: Don't worry, Tonya. We'll come up with something close. But, first we need a song.

TONYA: *(brightens)* Oh, right. That's easy. *(begins singing "O Christmas Tree," with the others joining her)*

MOTHER: Good job, Tonya! *(high five)* Since we already know the Bible doesn't have any Christmas trees, what does it have that's close?

TONYA: Does it have trees?

MOTHER: It certainly does. Can you think of one?

TONYA: Hey, I have one and a song to go with it! *(begins singing "Zacchaeus" and others join, emphasizing "the sycamore tree")*

MOTHER: Zacchaeus's story reminds me that we all need to meet Jesus personally. *(reads Luke 19:1–4)* Jesus makes it possible for everyone to know him. Do you remember how he did that?

TONYA: Yes, he died on the cross.

MOTHER: And that cross was made of?

ALL CHILDREN: Wood!

MOTHER: And wood comes from?

ALL CHILDREN: Trees!

MOTHER: You have it. *(high fives all around)* Christmas is just part of the story. Jesus came as a baby, but he came with a purpose. *(pause)* Looks like that is all our dough.

TONYA: All but the scraps.

MOTHER: Okay, roll the scraps and make round cookies with them. Then we're ready to put them in the oven.

Children form scraps of dough into cookies and place them on the cookie sheet.

TONY: You know what, Mom?

MOTHER: What?

TONY: We're pretty good at this.

MOTHER: Yes, you are.

TONY: Maybe we need to take this show on the road—you know, like a traveling dinner theater.

TAYLOR: Right! Only we'll be the traveling cookie show.

MOTHER: Before we hit the road, I think we need to hit this plate of freshly-baked cookies. What do you say?

TONY: Finally!

Lights out as each child grabs a baked cookie.

Not One Dime

by Diana C. Derringer

SUMMARY: *A child wishes for money to buy Christmas gifts. The child's friend offers a solution.*

CHARACTERS:
Child 1: boy or girl
Child 2: boy or girl

SETTING: *child's room*

PROPS: *scattered toys, books, markers, notebooks*

COSTUMES: *contemporary clothing*

Children play on the floor.

CHILD 1: *(enthusiastically)* Christmas is almost here.

CHILD 2: *(sadly)* Yeah, I know.

CHILD 1: What's wrong? Don't you like Christmas?

CHILD 2: Well, sure. Doesn't everybody?

CHILD 1: So, what's the problem, sour face?

CHILD 2: Well, you see, grownups have lots of gifts for us under the tree, but I don't have a thing for them—nothing —not a single gift.

CHILD 1: So?

CHILD 2: Don't you understand? Christmas is about giving, and I can't give anything.

CHILD 1: Why not? Just ask your mom for some money.

CHILD 2: *(sarcastically)* Yeah, right. I'm going to say, "Mom, I need some money so I can buy you a gift."

CHILD 1: Sounds like a good plan to me.

CHILD 2: Well, not to me.

CHILD 1: So, do you have a better plan?

CHILD 2: *(jumps up and starts pacing)* I don't know. I don't have any money or a credit card, or a checkbook, or a debit card, or a savings account. I don't have one thin dime! *(throws arms out)* What's a kid supposed to do?

CHILD 1: *(gets up and joins the pacing, forefinger under chin, then taps forehead)* Hmmm, let's see. What to do? What to do? This could be a real problem.

Child 1 and Child 2 continue pacing and thinking.

CHILD 1: *(excited)* I've got it! I've got it!

CHILD 2: What? Got what?

CHILD 1: You don't have to buy anything!

CHILD 2: *(irritated)* I just told you I do have to buy some gifts. I have to.

CHILD 1: I know you said you want to give some gifts. I'm saying you just don't have to buy them.

CHILD 2: Look, I'm not going to steal them. I don't want to spend Christmas in jail.

CHILD 1: No, you don't have to steal or do anything wrong, but you won't have to spend that one thin dime you don't have.

CHILD 2: That doesn't make sense. How can we give gifts if we don't spend money? Last time I checked, money really helps. And I don't think Mom or Dad would appreciate any of my worn-out toys.

CHILD 1: How about the gift of yourself?

CHILD 2: Huh?

CHILD 1: You know—the gift of yourself!

CHILD 2: No, I don't know. What do I do? Stick a bow on my head and sit under the tree? Besides, Mom and Dad already have plenty of me—sometimes way more than enough.

CHILD 1: I hear you on that. Why do you think I'm at your house today? Mom and Dad are enjoying a little p and q without me.

CHILD 2: P and q?

CHILD 1: You know, peace and quiet.

CHILD 2: Oh, okay. So what are you saying? Should I suddenly disappear for Christmas? They get a little fed up with me sometimes, but I think, deep down, they really like me.

CHILD 1: Here's the deal. What do your parents like for you to do?

CHILD 2: That's easy. They want me to do what they say.

CHILD 1: Oh, I know that, but what else?

CHILD 2: They really like it when I clean up this mess.

CHILD 1: Bingo!

CHILD 2: Bingo?

CHILD 1: Yeah, bingo. If your mom's like mine, she saves coupons for stores and restaurants. She loves to cash those things in for stuff. Right?

CHILD 2: *(puzzled)* Right.

CHILD 1: So, make your parents some "Me Coupons." *(points toward markers)* Hand me a marker and notebook. Let's get this show on the road. *(takes a marker and notebook from Child 2)* Let's see. You'll need a couple of coupons for cleaning your room, one for helping with other chores, one for a day without quarreling...

CHILD 2: A whole day?

CHILD 1: You can do it.

CHILD 2: Are you sure they will like this?

CHILD 1: Trust me. Grownups really get into this stuff. Why, I don't know, but they do. You might throw in a picture you draw. Oh, and be sure to write "I love you" on it. They really like that.

CHILD 2: So this giving of ourselves is a great gift?

CHILD 1: The best. After all, isn't that what Jesus did? Isn't that why we celebrate Christmas? Isn't that why we give gifts in the first place?

CHILD 2: How about that? I'm as rich as I can be, and I still don't have a dime.

Lights out as Child 1 and Child 2 begin making coupons.

The Wise Guys

by Diana C. Derringer

SUMMARY: *A child explains the role of the wise men who looked for Jesus.*

CHARACTER: *Child: boy or girl*

SETTING: *a family room*

PROPS: *a hand-size ceramic wise man*

COSTUME: *contemporary clothing*

The Child, holding the ceramic wise man, walks to center stage and faces the audience.

My friend Eric asked about our family's nativity scene. I was surprised, because Eric didn't know anything about it. Eric's family celebrates Christmas and everything. They have trees in every room, presents under the trees, reindeer in their yard, and Santa on their roof. But they don't have a nativity scene ... anywhere.

I thought that was a little strange. After all, Christmas is a celebration of Jesus' birthday. When I told Eric how Jesus was born in a manger, since none of the motels had a bed, he couldn't believe it. I explained that Jesus came to earth as our Savior. Eric thought I was joking. I told him, no, it was no joke. Then I reminded him what a mess our world is, with all the people fighting one another and everything. He decided maybe a Savior was a good idea after all.

Then I told Eric about the angels announcing Jesus' birth to the shepherds. He thought that was pretty cool. After all, it's not every day a guy's just hanging around and a bunch of angels show up.

But when I got to the wise guys, I had a harder time getting Eric to understand. I told him they lived real far away east of where Jesus was born, so they had to travel a long, long time. Eric asked why they were there with the newborn baby if they had such a long way to go. I told Eric that's a good question. We decided maybe the wise guys needed to be placed pretty far east of the nativity scene from now on. *(looks down at the wise man, then around the room)* So, now I have to decide which direction is east.

One thing about those guys. They knew to go where Jesus was, no matter how far they had to travel, how long it took, or which direction it was. Yep, definitely wise guys.

We've Never Heard

by Diana C. Derringer

SUMMARY: *Children from around the world describe themselves and their need to hear about Jesus.*

CHARACTERS:

Maria: eight-year-old girl from Colombia
Ahmed: seven-year boy from Syria
Aashi: ten-year-old girl from India
Ishmael: eleven-year-old boy from Sudan
Ya-Yu: nine-year-old girl from China
Kelsi: six-year-old girl from the United States
Children's choir
Reader: boy (offstage)

SETTING: *any*

PROPS: *none*

COSTUMES: *traditional clothing for countries listed, if available*

Children stand, evenly spaced, across the stage.

MARIA: My name is Maria. I'm eight years old. I live in Colombia. My father leads a rebel group. I'm not sure what happened to my mother. She disappeared when I was three. I have never heard about Jesus.

AHMED: My name is Ahmed. I'm seven years old. My family escaped the war in Syria. We paid a man all our money to ride in a crowded boat to Greece. We don't have a home anymore. I have never heard about Jesus.

AASHI: My name is Aashi. I'm ten years old. My family lives in India. We worship many gods and perform religious ceremonies to try to keep the gods happy with us. I have never heard about Jesus.

ISHMAEL: My name is Ishmael. I'm eleven years old. Soldiers attacked our village in Sudan. They killed most of the villagers, including my family. They forced me and other children to join their army. I miss my family. I have never heard about Jesus.

YA-YU: My name is Ya-Yu. I'm nine years old. I live in China. My parents say there is no God and religious people are weak. The government arrested one of our neighbors and put him in jail, because he held a church service in his apartment. I have never heard about Jesus.

KELSI: My name is Kelsi. I'm six years old. I live in the United States. My father is in jail for selling drugs. I live with my mommy and an uncle. He's not really my uncle, but that's what Mommy said to call him. They yell a lot and hit me sometimes. I get scared when they leave me alone. I have never heard about Jesus.

The children's choir moves behind the speakers. All sing "Go Tell It on the Mountain."

MARIA: *(steps forward)* Will you pray?

ISHMAEL: *(steps forward)* Will you give?

YA-YU: *(steps forward)* Will you go?

READER: "Then Jesus came to them and said, 'All authority in heaven and on earth has been given to me. Therefore go and make disciples of all nations, baptizing them in the name of the Father and of the Son and of the Holy Spirit, and teaching them to obey everything I have commanded you. And surely I am with you always, to the very end of the age'" (Matthew 28:18–20).

Lights out.

Yes, He Did

by Diana C. Derringer

SUMMARY: *A younger child eagerly agrees as an older child summarizes why Jesus came to earth.*

CHARACTERS:
Child 1: older boy or girl
Child 2: younger boy or girl

SETTING: *anywhere*

PROPS: *none*

COSTUMES: *contemporary clothing*

The two children stand near center stage. Child 2 responds with enthusiasm to everything Child 1 says.

CHILD 1: Jesus left his home in heaven.

CHILD 2: *(nods head)* Yes, he did.

CHILD 1: To be born a baby.

CHILD 2: *(nods head)* Yes, he did! *(moves arms for emphasis)* He really did!

CHILD 1: He was born in a manger.

CHILD 2: Yes, he was.

CHILD 1: But he didn't stay there.

CHILD 2: *(shakes head)* No, he didn't.

CHILD 1: He grew into a boy.

CHILD 2: *(nods head)* Yes, he did.

CHILD 1: He grew strong and smart.

CHILD 2: *(nods head, flexes muscles)* Yes, he did.

CHILD 1: Jesus became a great teacher.

CHILD 2: *(nods head)* Yes, he did.

CHILD 1: He helped hurting people.

CHILD 2: *(nods head)* Yes, he did.

CHILD 1: He died for our sins.

CHILD 2: *(nods head, looks sad)* Yes, he did.

CHILD 1: But he did not stay in the tomb.

CHILD 2: *(shakes head, eyes wide)* No, he didn't. He really didn't!

CHILD 1: After three days, Jesus rose from the dead.

CHILD 2: *(nods head)* Yes, he did! *(moves arms for emphasis)* He really did!

CHILD 1: Jesus defeated sin and death.

CHILD 2: *(nods head, smiles widely)* Yes, he did.

CHILD 1: He offers salvation to everyone.

CHILD 2: *(nods head)* Yes, he does.

CHILD 1: Will you accept Jesus' greatest gift?

CHILD 2: Yes, I will! I really will! *(turns to audience, extends arms)* Will you?

Youth

An Unexpected Savior

by Diana C. Derringer

SUMMARY: *Readers describe the unexpected way Jesus brought light to our dark world.*

CHARACTERS: *Five youth, male or female*

SETTING: *any location*

PROPS: *none*

COSTUMES: *contemporary clothing*

The youth stand, facing the audience, Youth 1 and 2 on one side, Youth 3 and 4 on the other, Youth 5 in the middle.

YOUTH 1: For centuries, our world has experienced

YOUTH 2: hatred,

YOUTH 3: abuse,

YOUTH 4: discrimination,

YOUTH 1: and evils too numerous to mention.

YOUTH 5: "They will look toward the earth and see only distress and darkness and fearful gloom, and they will be thrust into utter darkness."[1]

YOUTH 1: Yet, Jesus came into this damaged, hopeless mess, offering

YOUTH 2: love,

YOUTH 3: kindness,

YOUTH 4: unconditional acceptance,

YOUTH 1: and hope.

YOUTH 5: "The people walking in darkness have seen a great light; on those living in the land of deep darkness a light has dawned."[2]

YOUTH 1: Jesus did not come as a king on a throne.

YOUTH 2: He did not come as a warrior seeking revenge.

YOUTH 3: He did not come as a rich man hoarding his treasure.

YOUTH 4: He did not come as a strong man flaunting his power.

YOUTH 1: Jesus came as a baby, born to ordinary people, announced to lowly shepherds,

ALL YOUTH: Savior and servant of all.

YOUTH 5: "And there were shepherds living out in the fields nearby, keeping watch over their flocks at night. An angel of the Lord appeared to them, and the glory of the Lord shone around them, and they were terrified. But the angel said to them, 'Do not be afraid. I bring you good news that will cause great joy for all the people. Today in the town of David a Savior has been born to you; he is the Messiah, the Lord. This will be a sign to you: You will find a baby wrapped in cloths and lying in a manger.' Suddenly a great company of the heavenly host appeared with the angel, praising God and saying, 'Glory to God in the highest heaven, and on earth peace to those on whom his favor rests.' When the angels had left them and gone into heaven, the shepherds said to one another, 'Let's go to Bethlehem and see this thing that has happened, which the Lord has told us about.' So they hurried off and found Mary and Joseph, and the baby, who was lying in the manger."[3]

1 Isaiah 8:22

2 Isaiah 9:2

3 Luke 2:8–16

Christmas Carol

by Diana C. Derringer

SUMMARY: *A girl carries her love for Christmas to extremes for a reason.*

CHARACTER: *Carol: teen girl*

SETTING: *high school entry*

PROPS: *a Christmas tin filled with candy canes and Christmas cookies, mistletoe*

COSTUME: *gaudy Christmas clothing with at least one pocket*

DIRECTOR'S NOTES: *The name of a local high school can be substituted for Central High.*

Carol stands in the school entry, profile to the audience. She holds the tin of candy canes and cookies and has sprigs of mistletoe hanging from her pocket. She greets people with exaggerated enthusiasm as they arrive.

Good morning! Merry Christmas! Would you like a cookie or candy cane? Help yourself. They're free and a great way to start another exciting day at good old Central High. *(pause)* No? Not hungry? No problem. You have a great day anyway.

Good morning! Merry Christmas! Would you like a candy cane or cookie? They're free. *(pause)* Sure, help yourself to all you want. Take a couple for later.

(turns to audience, bounces with excitement) Don't you just love this time of year? The snow, the music, the excitement in the air?

(turns aside) Good morning! Merry Christmas! Would you like some ... Now that's what I like to see, someone with a hearty appetite and a smile on his face. You have a great day!

(turns to audience) As I was saying, don't you just love Christmas? The decorations, the cute clothes *(waves hand over her outfit)*, the movies.

(turns aside) Good morning! Merry Christmas! Would you like a candy cane or cookie to start the day? *(pause)* Oh, sorry, I didn't mean to mess with your diet. Here, *(reaches in pocket)* have a sprig of mistletoe instead.

(turns to audience) You know my favorite part of Christmas? The hope. Yep, the hope the season brings.

(turns aside) Good morning! Merry ... *(stumbles backward)* Oops, must be running late. *(calls out with hand to mouth)* .. Merry Christmas!

(turns to audience) I think maybe he could use an extra dose of Christmas cheer. I feel sorry for people who don't love Christmas.

(turns aside) Good morning! Merry Christmas! Would you like a candy cane or cookie to start your day? *(pause)* Well, thank you very much. I love to do it. *(tilts head)* Why do I do this? Do you really want to know? *(pause)* Okay, here goes. Christmas is a time of hope, and I want to share the hope I have with the rest of the world. Well, maybe I can't with the whole world, but Central High's a start. Anyway, Christmas celebrates Jesus coming into the world as our Savior. You

know how we all mess up sometimes. *(nods head)* Oh, don't I know it. It's hard for me to keep count of the mistakes I've made too. Anyway, our sins, the things we do wrong, separate us from God. But God loves us enough that Jesus came into the world to take the punishment for our sins. That's what Jesus did when he died on the cross. But, thank God for Easter, our celebration that Jesus rose from the dead after three days, conquering sin and death. When we confess our sins to God and ask Jesus to take control of our lives, he forgives our sins, guides us with his Holy Spirit, and promises us a home in heaven. Let me tell you, life doesn't get any better than that. So, that's the reason I do this. I love the hope of Christmas, because it points us to the promise of Easter. *(pause)* You're welcome. Let me know if you want to talk more. My name's Carol. *(pause)* Thank you! Merry Christmas to you too!

Lights out.

Dashing Through the Mall

by Diana C. Derringer

SUMMARY: *Two girls recognize the need to change their spending habits.*

CHARACTERS:
Youth 1: girl
Youth 2: girl

SETTING: *a shopping mall*

PROPS: *several stuffed shopping bags*

COSTUMES: *contemporary clothing*

The two youth, carrying multiple shopping bags, enter from opposite sides of the stage and meet in the middle.

YOUTH 1: *(sings and swings her bags in time to the tune of "Dashing through the Snow.")* Jingle bells, the latest sales, new jeans all the way.

YOUTH 2: Hey there! What are you doing?

YOUTH 1: *(still swinging bags in time to the music)* What does it look like I'm doing? I'm getting into the Christmas spirit!

YOUTH 2: Sounds to me like you're making a list and checking it twice.

YOUTH 1: Well, yeah! Isn't that what Christmas is all about? *(sings again)* Getting, getting, getting, getting, getting all the way, hey!

YOUTH 2: *(shakes head)* Oh, please.

YOUTH 1: Oh, please, what? Your bags are as full as mine, and I bet most of that is for yourself.

YOUTH 2: Well ...

YOUTH 1: Well, what? Am I right or not?

YOUTH 2: Well, okay, okay, yeah, most of it's for me, but it's stuff I really need.

YOUTH 1: *(digs in Youth 2's bags)* Yep, you definitely need two more sweaters to add to the fifteen you already own. Oh, and for sure you need new boots. It's only been, what, two weeks since you bought your last pair?

YOUTH 2: *(slightly irritated)* You don't have to get all nasty about it. Besides, you're just as guilty as I am. *(pleads)* But please don't tell Ms. Kym, especially not after last Sunday's lesson.

YOUTH 1: What lesson? I sorta' slept in.

YOUTH 2: Our focus verse was "It is more blessed to give than to receive."[1] Ms. Kym talked about how Jesus gave up his home in heaven to offer us the gift of salvation. Since he gave his life for us, she asked if we shouldn't be willing to make some sacrifices for him and others.

YOUTH 1: Ouch!

YOUTH 2: Ouch is right. We divided into groups to talk about ways we could spend our money better, so we have more to give to missions and local ministries. Guess who opened her big mouth and said we could spend less on clothes.

YOUTH 1: Oh boy, I think I'm coming down with a bad case of guilt, too, and I wasn't even there.

YOUTH 2: You should have been. It was a really good lesson.

YOUTH 1: If it was such a great lesson, what are you doing here?

YOUTH 2: Good question. *(pause)* You don't know it, girl, but you just became my accountability partner.

YOUTH 1: Your what?

YOUTH 2: Ms. Kym suggested everyone get an accountability partner—someone to be sure we act like we should and to kind of rein us in when we get out of line.

YOUTH 1: Aha. So does that mean you become my accountability partner too?

YOUTH 2: Afraid so, my friend.

YOUTH 1: Hmmm. So I guess the first thing we need to do is take some of this stuff back and put money in next week's mission offering. Whadda' say, partner?

YOUTH 1 AND 2: *(exit, singing)* Dashing through the mall, with refunds on the way, out the door we go, we'll save some cash today. Hey!

---

1 Acts 20:35

Sing That Song

by Diana C. Derringer

SUMMARY: *Game show contestants identify and sing Christmas songs.*

CHARACTERS:
Charlie B: boy master of ceremonies
Linda: girl contestant
Laci: girl contestant
Ryder: boy contestant

SETTING: *television broadcasting set*

PROPS: *four podiums, three Christmas bells, a small stuffed dog*

COSTUMES: *tacky Christmas outfits*

Contestants stand behind podiums on the right side of the stage. A Christmas bell sits on each contestant's podium. Charlie B enters and moves behind his podium on the left side of the stage.

CHARLIE B.: Good evening, ladies and gentlemen, and welcome to the first Christmas program for "Sing that Song!" Let's get started by meeting tonight's contestants. *(steps in front of Linda's podium)* First we have Linda, a young lady who admits she's still working on a few insecurities. As a result, we gladly honored her request to bring a favorite stuffed animal to tonight's program. Welcome, Linda!

LINDA: *(timid, clutches stuffed dog to her chest)* Thank you, Charlie B. I'm thrilled to be here.

CHARLIE B: As we are to have you here, Linda. *(steps in front of Laci's podium)* Next we have Laci, a student who knows what she wants and says she usually gets it. Laci hopes to become a psychiatrist after she completes her education. Glad to have you on the show, Laci.

LACI: *(loudly)* Glad to be here, Charlie B. *(glaring at Charlie B)* Nothing wrong with following a person's dreams, is there? After all, the world is filled with enough wimps already *(looks at Linda, who looks down in embarrassment)* And, just so you know, I have every intention of walking away with tonight's prize. *(grabs Charlie B's collar)* Got that, Charlie B?

CHARLIE B: *(startled, moves Laci's hand from his collar)* Good grief! Ahem ... I mean ... yes ... well ... welcome, Laci. *(steps in front of Ryder's podium)* And now for our final contestant this evening, we have Ryder, a fan of Beethoven since preschool. He hopes to major in music with a piano emphasis. Welcome, Ryder.

RYDER: Thanks, Charlie B. *(looks down at hands and wiggles fingers)*

CHARLIE B: *(pause)* Ah! A man of few words. *(glances at Laci)* I like that. *(turns to audience and claps hands)* Audience, please join me in a round of applause for tonight's contestants. *(returns to his podium)* As you know, contestants, we replaced buzzers with Christmas bells for the month of December. I will give you the clue to a song. The first person to ring your bell answers the question. You must give the correct song title and then sing that song. If you fail to respond correctly, another contestant can then try. Are you ready?

Contestants nod.

CHARLIE B: Okay! Let's get started. Here's your first clue: A holiday plant.

LACI: *(yells)* I've got it! I've got it!

CHARLIE B: Remember, contestants, you must first ring your bell.

Ryder rings bell.

LACI: Rats!

CHARLIE B: Yes, Ryder?

RYDER: "O Christmas Tree."

CHARLIE B: That's absolutely right. One point for Ryder. Now, for the bonus, can you *(louder, with exaggerated emphasis)* sing that song?

Ryder sings. Laci glares at Ryder.

CHARLIE: *(clears throat)* Moving right along to our next clue: Happiness around the globe.

Laci grabs for her bell, knocks it to the floor, picks up the bell, and hits her head on the podium when she stands. Linda softly rings her bell.

CHARLIE B: Your answer, Linda?

LACI: *(angrily)* But, I had the answer!

CHARLIE B: I'm sure you did, Laci, but rules are rules. Now, Linda, your answer, please.

Laci mutters and glares at Charlie B and Linda.

LINDA: "Joy to the World."

CHARLIE B: That's right, Linda! For the bonus, please *(louder, with exaggerated emphasis)* sing that song!

Linda sings. Laci glares, crosses her arms, and pouts.

CHARLIE B: We now have a tie between Ryder and Linda. Here's our next clue: A cold statue of precipitation.

LACI: *(grabs bell, rings wildly, and shouts)* "Frosty the Snowman!"

CHARLIE B: Absolutely, Laci. Now *(louder with exaggerated emphasis)* sing that song!

Laci sings loudly and dramatically.

CHARLIE B: Wow, folks! We have a three-way tie. Here comes our tie-breaker: A special evening.

Linda timidly rings bell while Laci reaches for hers.

LACI: Rats! Double rats!

CHARLIE B: No pressure, Linda, but if you can name and sing that song, you will be our grand prize winner tonight.

LINDA: *(timid, clutches stuffed dog closer)* "O Holy Night"?

CHARLIE B: You have it, Linda. Can you *(louder, with exaggerated emphasis)* sing that song?

Linda sets her stuffed dog on the podium and steps in front of the podium. Lights dim, with a spotlight on Linda, who reverently sings. Everyone, including Laci, watches in awe.

LINDA: *(softly but confidently)* That, Charlie B, is the reason we celebrate Christmas.

Lights out.

To the Manger and Back

by Diana C. Derringer

SUMMARY: *Imagine traveling back in time to the night of Jesus' birth. These two young people manage that feat. What they discover surprises them.*

CHARACTERS:
Youth 1: male or female
Youth 2: male or female

SETTING 1 AND 3: *a family room*

SETTING 2: *a stable in Bethlehem*

PROPS: *two comfortable chairs, nativity scene, pillow, manger*

COSTUMES: *contemporary clothing*

Scene 1

The two youth lounge in chairs, legs over the arms, talking. The nativity scene sits in the background between them.

YOUTH 1: You gonna' be in the Christmas play this year?

YOUTH 2: Yeah, I think so. Parts haven't been assigned yet, but I signed up for it. Are you?

YOUTH 1: I don't know yet. I mean, it's the same old thing every year—Mary, Joseph, and baby Jesus in a manger. The shepherds visit. The wise men visit, even though they didn't actually get there probably for two years. We really need to get that part fixed, you know.

YOUTH 2: Huh, I didn't know that. Are you sure?

YOUTH 1: Pretty sure. See, the wise men traveled a long distance from the east, so no way could they have made it that night. Plus, the Bible says the wise men visited a child in a house, not a baby in a manger. Plus, old King Herod had all the little boys under age 2 killed when he heard about Jesus from the wise men. Evidence presented. Case closed.

YOUTH 2: Okay, okay. Thank you, counselor, for today's court case.

YOUTH 1: Sometimes I get really strange thoughts.

YOUTH 2: *(exaggerated surprise)* Oh, really? Now, who would have thought that?

YOUTH 1: *(throws a pillow at Youth 2)* You don't have to get all smart on me. But think about it: wouldn't it have been cool to actually be there the night Jesus was born?

YOUTH 2: *(hesitantly)* I guess. I never really thought about it.

YOUTH 1: I mean, can you imagine getting to see Jesus as a baby, to hold and maybe rock him, and to meet Mary and Joseph and the shepherds, minus the wise men?

YOUTH 2: I suppose so. *(looks toward nativity scene)* All the nativity scenes make it seem so peaceful—such a special moment. Wow, I guess that would be pretty cool.

Music plays. Lights out.

Scene 2

Manger sits center stage. Youth 1 and 2 enter from one side, looking around.

YOUTH 1: Where are we?

YOUTH 2: Beats me. One minute we were at your house talking, and now we're ... *(pause)* here. How did that happen?

YOUTH 1: I don't know. I mean, there we were talking about how cool it would have been to be present when Jesus was born. *(stops quickly, backs up)* Whoa, now! Wait a minute! This is getting way too weird.

YOUTH 2: What? *(pause, then louder)* What?

YOUTH 1: No way. It can't be. *(calmer)* I'm just letting my imagination get the best of me. *(grabs Youth 2's arm)* Come on. Let's figure out where we are and what's going on.

YOUTH 2: Whatever you say. By the way, I don't have a clue what you're talking about.

YOUTH 1: You never do! Quite honestly, neither do I, but come on.

YOUTH 2: *(walks toward the manger)* What in the world is that smell?

YOUTH 1: Gross! If I didn't know better, I'd say somebody had a bad case of diarrhea.

YOUTH 2: Gag! The closer we get to that shelter, the worse it gets.

YOUTH 1: Well, hold your nose, we're going in! *(grabs Youth 2 and ducks as though going through an entrance just before the manger)*

YOUTH 2: *(looks around)* Now we know the source of the smell. Or should I say sources? I've never seen cows and sheep up close, have you?

YOUTH 1: Better watch where you step, mate, if you don't want the smell on you.

YOUTH 2: That's not all we need to watch. Look at those scruffy looking dudes just ahead.

YOUTH 1: I wouldn't want to meet them on a dark night. Oops! Come to think of it, this is a dark night. From the looks of them, I doubt they smell much better than the cows.

YOUTH 2: *(lowers voice)* Watch your mouth! I'm in no mood for getting the stuffing beat out of me.

YOUTH 1: *(irritated)* Alright already. What do they see anyway, and why are they getting on their knees?

YOUTH 2: *(stands on toes)* Hey, look! It's a baby!

YOUTH 1: I was right! It's him!

YOUTH 2: What are you talking about? It's him who?

YOUTH 1: The baby, goofball, the baby. Remember how I said it would be cool to be present at Jesus' birth? Well, I don't know how it happened or what's going on, but somehow we're there.

YOUTH 2: You mean there, like there.

YOUTH 1: That's exactly what I mean. Look around. You've got a stable with cows and sheep. You've got shepherds with sticks.

YOUTH 2: Staffs.

YOUTH 1: Sticks, staffs, whatever. You've got a young girl next to the manger and an older guy next to her. You've got shepherds on their knees in front of the baby. What more do you want?

YOUTH 2: Right now, I'd like a comfortable place to sit, but those seem in short supply.

YOUTH 1: Take your pick: the ground, the ground covered with hay, or the ground covered with what we smelled several yards back.

YOUTH 2: Thanks. I'll pass. I'd rather not join the pint-sized creatures crawling around down there.

YOUTH 1: A bit different from our nativity scenes at home, huh?

YOUTH 2: You got that right. It's stinky, dirty, dusty, and buggy. The shepherds could use a good soak too.

YOUTH 1: I doubt they have many showers where they work.

YOUTH 2: Good point.

YOUTH 1: I knew Jesus humbled himself to come to earth. I guess I never thought about just how humble his birth was.

Youth 1 and 2 step closer to the manger and fall to their knees. Lights out.

Scene 3
Youth 1 and 2 rest on their knees before the nativity scene.

Adults

Christmas Without Papa

by Diana C. Derringer

SUMMARY: *A family considers skipping Christmas due to their Papa's death.*

CHARACTERS:
Mama: older woman
Alex: adult male
Debbie: adult female
Autumn: small girl

SETTING: *a family room*

PROPS: *couch, two chairs, facial tissues on the edge of a coffee table, coloring book, crayons*

COSTUMES: *dark contemporary clothing*

Adults sit on the couch and chairs, talking. Mama looks down, hands clutched, occasionally dabbing her eyes. Autumn sits on the floor, coloring in her book on the coffee table.

DEBBIE: *(reaches for a tissue, voice breaks)* I can't believe he's gone. Papa was always healthy as a horse.

ALEX: He worked like a horse too.

AUTUMN: *(quietly, head still down)* Papa's not a horse.

DEBBIE: *(leans forward and hugs Autumn)* Of course, Papa's not a horse, Autumn. We're just saying he looked healthy and worked hard.

AUTUMN: *(never looking up)* But, Papa died.

DEBBIE: Yes, honey, Papa died.

AUTUMN: And now he's in heaven.

DEBBIE: *(dabs tissue to eyes)* Yes, Papa's in heaven.

AUTUMN: And we're sad.

DEBBIE: Yes, we're sad, because we miss Papa. But we're also happy that Papa's with Jesus, and we'll see him again someday.

ALEX: Debbie, what are we going to do about Christmas this year?

DEBBIE: Oh, Alex, I can't stand the thought of having our usual Christmas without Papa.

ALEX: It would be tough alright.

DEBBIE: And just two weeks away. Papa always took such an active role.

ALEX: Nobody could roast a turkey like Papa.

DEBBIE: Or lead Christmas carols.

ALEX: And Papa always read Luke's Christmas story.

DEBBIE: He hung the stockings and placed the star on the tree.

ALEX: Christmas just won't be Christmas without him.

AUTUMN: *(quietly, never looking up)* Yes, it will.

ALEX: What did you say, honey?

AUTUMN: I said yes, it will.

ALEX: Yes, it will what?

AUTUMN: Christmas will be Christmas without Papa.

ALEX: Why, sure it will. We just won't have our family Christmas like we usually do, since we miss Papa so much.

AUTUMN: Why not?

ALEX: Because we're so sad.

AUTUMN: But, I'm sad anyway, and I'll be sadder not doing what Papa liked. *(looks up, emphatic)* I don't think Papa would like your plan.

DEBBIE: What makes you say that, Autumn?

AUTUMN: *(lays crayon down, stands, starts to cry)* Cause Papa loved Christmas, and he loved for us to love Christmas.

DEBBIE: *(pulls Autumn into her lap, dabs eyes)* That's true, sweetie.

AUTUMN: *(wiggles free and stands again)* What Papa loved most about Christmas was seeing us having a good time celebrating Jesus' birth *(hands on hips)* together. *(looks from one adult to the other)* Isn't that what Christmas is all about—celebrating Jesus?

ALEX: *(clears throat)* Yes, it is, Autumn.

AUTUMN: Jesus still came, didn't he?

ALEX: Yes, he did.

AUTUMN: Jesus is still in heaven, isn't he?

ALEX: Yes, he is.

AUTUMN: Papa's celebrating every day with Jesus, isn't he?

ALEX: Indeed, he is.

AUTUMN: We'll miss Papa wherever we are, won't we?

ALEX: *(clears throat)* Yes, we will.

AUTUMN: So, can we please miss him together? *(throws herself into Debbie's lap and starts crying)*

MAMA: *(looks up and smiles at Autumn)* She has a point, you know. If your sweet Papa were here, he'd say it's okay to be sad, but it's not okay to skip our family Christmas. We can change it around a bit, start some new traditions. Maybe we can have a time to share our favorite Christmas memories with Papa and just cry buckets of tears. Really, that might be just what we need. But, Autumn's right. Jesus came, and Jesus reigns. We need to keep telling the world, and the world starts here at home. Autumn said it well. Christmas is about Jesus, not Papa.

Autumn crawls in Mama's lap, hugs her neck, and smiles. Adults reach for tissues. Lights out.

Have You Heard

by Diana C. Derringer

SUMMARY: *Carolers plan to skip the home of a pregnant teen-age girl until they recall details of the first Christmas.*

CHARACTERS:
Caroler 1: male
Caroler 2: female
Caroler 3: female
Caroler 4: male

SETTING: *cold evening outside*

PROPS: *songbooks or sheet music*

COSTUMES: *warm winter clothing*

Carolers stand on one side of the stage. They sing a Christmas carol, wave, call Merry Christmas, and move to center stage.

CAROLER 1: Okay, gang, on to the next house.

CAROLER 2: *(stomps feet)* Wait a minute. I think my toes froze to the ground.

CAROLER 3: I know what you mean. *(flexes fingers)* I may never have feeling in my fingers again.

CAROLER 4: I have you both beat. *(rubs the end of his nose* *with the back of his hand)* My nose is so cold, I can't tell if it's dripping.

CAROLER 1: Trust me, man. I'll tell you if that happens!

Everyone laughs.

CAROLER 3: Just think. We could be in a nice warm mall Christmas shopping.

CAROLER 4: *(mock horror)* Thanks, but no thanks. I'd rather freeze to death with icicles hanging from my nose!

CAROLER 1: You have to admit, hot chocolate from the food court doesn't sound bad.

CAROLER 4: If we're eating, I say let's go whole hog. I'll take a double bacon cheeseburger with curly fries and a large mocha shake, followed by a double chocolate brownie.

CAROLER 3: *(concerned)* Heart attack heaven, man. You have to start eating better.

CAROLER 4: Okay. Okay. But remind me after the first of the year. I think Marcie's getting me a treadmill for Christmas anyway.

CAROLER 2: Just what the doctor ordered.

CAROLER 4: Believe me, it wasn't my idea.

CAROLER 1: Let's keep moving, guys, or we'll never finish.

CAROLER 2: *(almost whispers)* We might want to skip this next house.

CAROLER 1: Why? Who lives there?

CAROLER 2: Haven't you heard? Well, *(looks around again)* you remember that family that joined our church a few months ago—the one with those rowdy teens?

CAROLER 4: Who could forget them? Although, that one girl wasn't too bad—rather quiet, in fact.

CAROLER 2: If you've noticed, she hasn't been to church the last few weeks. I heard she was engaged to some older guy, but now she's pregnant and due any time. The guy plans to dump her. Says the baby isn't his.

CAROLER 4: Poor girl.

CAROLER 3: What do you mean poor girl? I say poor guy.

CAROLER 4: It's a sad situation for everyone, if you ask me.

CAROLER 2: Sad situation or not, I wonder if maybe we shouldn't just skip them.

CAROLER 3: That sounds like a good plan to me. Let's go.

CAROLER 1: Wait a minute, everybody. Let's think this thing through. We don't know her circumstances for sure, right?

CAROLER 2: Well, no, but I have it on good authority...

CAROLER 1: Sometimes our good authorities get their facts wrong. And regardless of what's going on, this family needs God's love and our love now more than ever. *(pause)* Plus, if I recall correctly, they're not the first family to face this.

CAROLER 3: I know. Isn't it awful how commonplace it's become?

CAROLER 2: Poor babies hardly have a chance.

CAROLER 1: Actually, I was thinking more about two thousand years ago. Don't you imagine this is the way people in Nazareth talked about Mary and Joseph? Can't you hear their neighbors whispering, "Have you heard?"

CAROLER 3: Oh dear! I never thought of it that way.

CAROLER 1: Most of us don't. All Mary's neighbors knew was that she was engaged to an older man and became pregnant. Joseph planned to break their engagement, because he knew the baby wasn't his. Imagine how both must have felt and what everyone in Nazareth was saying.

CAROLER 2: *(near tears)* I'm so sorry. I know better than to carry tales, but I do it without thinking. I remember Pastor Mike said Mary could have been stoned for adultery. I may not have thrown physical stones at this poor girl, but I certainly have thrown some verbal ones. I'm so, so sorry.

CAROLER 1: *(pats Caroler 2's shoulder)* We're all guilty of doing things we know we shouldn't or failing to do things we should. Isn't that the reason Jesus came?

CAROLER 2: Well, this frozen body has had a warm change of heart. Let's give this young lady and her family a good dose of Christmas cheer and let her know we've missed her. I've received God's love and forgiveness. It's about time I share them.

Carolers walk and sing "We Wish You a Merry Christmas."

Paradoxical Peace

by Diana C. Derringer

SUMMARY: *Readers contrast Jesus' promise of peace with the world's lack of peace.*

CHARACTERS: *Four readers, male or female*

SETTING: *any*

PROPS: *none*

COSTUMES: *contemporary clothing*

Readers 1 and 4 stand on one side of the stage. Readers 2 and 3 stand on the opposite side.

READER 1: "For to us a child is born, to us a son is given, and the government will be on his shoulders. And he will be called Wonderful Counselor, Mighty God, Everlasting Father, Prince of Peace."[1]

READER 2: We read, sing, and dream of peace on earth. Yet, never in the history of our world have we known earthly peace.

READER 3: Nations fight nations. Ethnic groups throw slurs, stones, and worse. Families ignore commitments, ridding themselves of one another as easily as they discard old clothes. Teams replace teamwork with a me-first attitude.

READER 2: Workers undermine bosses and co-workers. Politicians split into "us" versus "them," creating havoc for the governments and people they were elected to serve. Courtrooms overflow with a never-ending stream of lawlessness and contempt. Even churches fight without and within.

READER 3: Such constant blaming, bickering, and breaking down of relationships make the celebration of peace questionable.

READER 4: Nevertheless, Isaiah and Zechariah prophesied peace in the Old Testament. Luke detailed the angels' proclamation of peace in the New Testament. In spite of our world's distress, their words remain as relevant today as the night of Jesus' birth.

READER 1: Everyone who experiences God's salvation knows peace that transcends any circumstance. Paul said in Ephesians 2:14, Jesus is our peace. When we allow Jesus' presence to reign in our lives, we enjoy true peace, whether the world around us is peaceful or not.

READER 4: When we hurt, Jesus' peace eases our pain. When we face death, his peace provides comfort and reassurance. When we endure abuse, he wraps us in his arms of peace. When darkness engulfs us, we walk by the light of his peace.

READER 1: When persecuted for our faith, we can respond with and proclaim his peace. When we fall flat in failure, he picks us up, dusts us off, and tells us to try again—to go in his peace.

READER 4: We celebrate daily the peace made possible through God's all-sufficient gift of grace.

READER 1: We look forward to the everlasting peace Jesus will usher in at his return. All conflict and pain will disappear for those who follow him.

ALL: We cannot know peace on our own. Only when we confess Jesus as Lord will he cover us in his peace and grant us the power to live it.

---

1 Isaiah 9:6

Poor Little Baby

by Diana C. Derringer

SUMMARY: *A couple discuss meeting Mary and Joseph near Bethlehem.*

CHARACTERS:
Jacob: adult male
Elizabeth: adult female
Reader: male or female (offstage)

SETTING: *a Bethlehem inn*

PROPS: *a floor mat*

COSTUMES: *long tunics and head coverings*

The couple sits on the mat mid-stage.

ELIZABETH: Whew! Finally we found a place to stay. I can't believe that many inns had no vacancies.

JACOB: I knew it would be bad, but I never expected this.

ELIZABETH: I don't know if my poor feet will ever be the same.

JACOB: Ah, but you rode the donkey most of our journey, Elizabeth. How do you think my feet feel?

ELIZABETH: You're right, Jacob. Thank you for treating me like a queen. *(looks up)* And thank you, God, for a place to lay our heads.

JACOB: *(looks up)* Plus food to eat and a safe journey. *(looks at Elizabeth)* I feel sorry for anyone still searching for shelter.

ELIZABETH: *(shakes her head)* Don't I know it? I wonder what happened to that poor couple we met earlier today.

JACOB: The one with a baby on the way?

ELIZABETH: If I know anything about babies, and I should with five of my own, that baby will be here soon. Bless that poor mother's heart. I hope they found a room.

JACOB: I doubt they did, Elizabeth. We passed them early this morning, so they probably didn't reach Bethlehem until the last hour or so.

ELIZABETH: Poor girl. She has to be exhausted. Mark my words: room or no room, that baby will be born tonight.

JACOB: *(shakes his head)* What a way to enter the world. I hope he's not born on the streets.

ELIZABETH: What makes you so sure it's a boy?

JACOB: I don't know. They seemed certain.

ELIZABETH: Bless his poor little heart. I hope his life on earth is better than his birth.

Lights out, followed by reading of Isaiah 53.

The Christmas Visit

by Diana C. Derringer

SUMMARY: *A woman, overwhelmed with problems, pours out her heart in prayer.*

CHARACTERS:
Woman: middle-aged
Reader: male (offstage)
Carolers

SETTING: *a family room*

PROPS: *small Christmas tree with flashing lights, loveseat, doorbell, food containers, boxes wrapped like gifts, a tricycle*

COSTUMES: *contemporary clothing*

Woman kneels in front of the loveseat, crying as she prays. Christmas tree lights flash in the background.

WOMAN: Dear God, you said you would never give us more than we can bear, but I don't think I can handle much more. I'm so tired. *(voice catches)*

READER: "Come to me, all you who are weary and burdened, and I will give you rest."[1]

WOMAN: What will I do without Ron? I hate to see him suffer, but he's the only man I've ever loved. We've been sweethearts since second grade. I know it's selfish, but I don't want to let him go.

READER: "'He will wipe every tear from their eyes. There will be no more death' or mourning or crying or pain, for the old order of things has passed away."[2]

WOMAN: How will I pay for all this? Hospital bills, nurses and doctors, therapy, equipment, and pills—the stack keeps growing, and Ron hasn't worked for two years. Now I can't work, and I don't know if I'll still have a job when ... when ... *(sobs)* when he's gone.

READER: "Therefore I tell you, do not worry about your life, what you will eat; or about your body, what you will wear. For life is more than food, and the body more than clothes. Consider the ravens: They do not sow or reap, they have no storeroom or barn; yet God feeds them. And how much more valuable you are than birds! Who of you by worrying can add a single hour to your life?[3]

WOMAN: And what's going to happen with Ron, Jr.? What will it take for him to turn his life around? Where did we go wrong?

READER: "Trust in the LORD with all your heart and lean not on your own understanding; in all your ways submit to him, and he will make your paths straight."[4]

WOMAN: And Ron Jr.'s children? They love their daddy, but his life's so messed up. Christmas is almost here, and I haven't bought a single gift.

READER: "If you ... know how to give good gifts to your children, how much more will your Father in heaven give good gifts to those who ask him!"[5]

WOMAN: God, how will I make it alone?

READER: "Never will I leave you; never will I forsake you."[6]

WOMAN: *(desperately)* Are you there, God? Do you hear me? I want to trust you. I want to believe. Help me, Lord.

READER: "Ask and it will be given to you; seek and you will find; knock and the door will be opened to you."[7]

WOMAN: Please, God, I need peace. Please help me know you care.

READER: "For to us a child is born, to us a son is given, and the government will be on his shoulders. And he will be called Wonderful Counselor, Mighty God, Everlasting Father, Prince of Peace."[8] *(pause)* "In this world you will have trouble. But take heart! I have overcome the world."[9]

A doorbell sounds. The woman rises and opens the door. Carolers enter, carrying food and gifts, pushing a tricycle. They sing the first verse of "Hark! the Herald Angels Sing."

READER: "Love one another. As I have loved you, so you must love one another. By this everyone will know that you are my disciples, if you love one another."[10]

Lights out.

---

1 Matthew 11:28

2 Revelation 21:4

3 Luke 12:22–25

4 Proverbs 3:5–6

5 Matthew 7:11

6 Hebrews 13:5

7 Matthew 7:7

8 Isaiah 9:6

9 John 16:33

10 John 13:34–35

General

Forgiveness

by Paul Shepherd

SUMMARY: *A father struggles to forgive his sons for a forgotten argument.*

CHARACTERS:
Mother: older woman
Father: older man
Son 1: young adult male
Son 2: young adult male

SETTING: *a living room at one house (one side of stage) and a dining room at another house (opposite side of stage).*

PROPS: *Christmas tree, five ornaments, recliner, two chairs and a table, two coffee cups, two cell phones, magazine*

COSTUMES: *contemporary clothing*

Scene 1

MOTHER: *(placing ornaments on tree)* You know, it's been five years since we've had the family here for Christmas.

FATHER: Really?

MOTHER: Yes. Five years. Don't you miss having the family together like we did when the boys were young and the grandkids were babies?

FATHER: I hadn't really thought about it.

MOTHER: Seriously? I think about it all the time, especially when I put up the tree. Those boys used to be right under my feet helping me place the ornaments. Don't you remember? And, the first years of the grandbabies when we bought special gifts for them. You remember?

FATHER: Vaguely.

MOTHER: I know you. You pretend it doesn't bother you but I know better. Can't you guys just figure this out and let's move on?

FATHER: All they have to do is apologize for what they said and we could.

MOTHER: So, you're just going to go on with this?

FATHER: Until they call.

Scene 2

SON 1: Almost Christmas.

SON 2: I know. Used to be my favorite time of year until the big blow up at Dad's.

SON 1: That was bad. Still remember him storming out of the house and driving off in a huff.

SON 2: Yeah. I'd never seen him that upset. Do you remember what happened?

SON 1: Not really. We were just talking, discussing I guess, and he erupted. Wow.

SON 2: How long has that been?

SON 1: Five years I think. Can you believe it?

Scene 3

MOTHER: *(continuing to decorate the tree)* Do you even remember what was the big deal?

FATHER: Doesn't matter.

MOTHER: Sure it matters. Someone has to be the bigger man and break the ice. *Someone.* By the way, I remember right after we were married and you and your Dad had an argument. You didn't talk to him for years. Then one day, he called. Said he was sorry and missed you … and me. Hmm.

(Father closes the magazine)

MOTHER: Surely, at Christmas time when we celebrate Jesus and his birth, you could be the one who calls. We talk all the time at church about Jesus and how his love teaches us to turn the other cheek and forgive. What a gift it would be, for both of us, and for them, if you would call and heal the wounds.

FATHER: *(turns and looks at Mother)*

Scene 4

SON 1: I wonder what he would do if we just called and said we're sorry.

SON 2: Probably hang up.

SON 1: Maybe, but maybe not. You want to try?

SON 2: Let's call.

Scene 5

FATHER: You know, you're right. I can't even remember why I got upset. Foolish. I know better and we've missed five years of celebration and memories. I read my Bible and know the right thing to do. What would Jesus do?

MOTHER: Get your phone and call. I know they'd love to hear your voice.

(Father picks up phone at the same time Son 1 calls)

SON 1: Dad?

FATHER: Hi, Son, I want…

SON 1: Dad, we've been talking and…

FATHER: No, wait. Let me talk. I want to tell you how sorry I am and how much I've missed you all. I want you to come home for Christmas and we can put all this behind us.

SON 1: Dad. Thanks for calling. We've missed you too. Life's too short to miss this special time.

FATHER: I haven't done what I've preached to you boys all these years and what I know Jesus would want me to do. Christmas is about his birth and the story he brings to all of us—love and forgiveness and doing the right thing. Can you forgive me?

SON 1: Nothing to forgive. See you on Christmas.

The End

12 Days of Christmas, Jesus Said to Me

by Paul Shepherd

SUMMARY: *Singers will sing to the tune of 12 Days of Christmas, repeating their words as words given to them by Jesus.*

CHARACTERS: *12 people of all ages*

SETTING: *none*

PROPS: *none*

COSTUMES: *none*

Singers may line up on stage facing the congregation. Accompaniment may or may not be used. Each singer may sing their respective "day" when it comes around as the main verse and each time it's repeated, or alternatively, each person may sing one full verse.

On the first day of Christmas, Jesus said to me:
I'll give you life eternally.

On the second day of Christmas, Jesus said to me:
Grace is for you,
And, I'll give you life eternally.

On the third day of Christmas, Jesus said to me:
Do not fear,
Grace is for you,
And, I'll give you life eternally.

On the fourth day of Christmas, Jesus said to me:
Patient and kind,
Do not fear,
Grace is for you,
And, I'll give you life eternally.

On the fifth day of Christmas, Jesus said to me:
Love....Peace...and Joy....
Patient and kind,
Do not fear,
Grace is for you,
And, I'll give you life eternally.

On the sixth day of Christmas, Jesus said to me:
Honor your parents,
Love....Peace...and Joy...
Patient and kind,
Do not fear,
Grace is for you,
And, I'll give you life eternally.

On the seventh day of Christmas, Jesus said to me:
Love's always with you,
Honor your parents,
Love...Peace...and Joy...
Patient and kind,
Do not fear,
Grace is for you,
And, I'll give you life eternally.

On the eighth day of Christmas, Jesus said to me:
You're now forgiven,
Love's always with you,
Honor your parents,
Love…Peace….and Joy…
Patient and kind,
Do not fear,
Grace is for you,
And, I'll give you life eternally.

On the ninth day of Christmas, Jesus said to me:
Make choices wisely,
You're now forgiven,
Love's always with you,
Honor your parents,
Love…Peace….and Joy…
Patient and kind,
Do not fear,
Grace is for you,
And, I'll give you life eternally.

On the tenth day of Christmas, Jesus said to me:
Share love with others,
Make choices wisely,
You're now forgiven,
Love's always with you,
Honor your parents,
Love…Peace….and Joy…
Patient and kind,
Do not fear,
Grace is for you,
And, I'll give you life eternally.

On the eleventh day of Christmas Jesus said to me:

Be a cheerful giver,
Share love with others,
Make choices wisely,
You're now forgiven,
Love's always with you,
Honor your parents,
Love…Peace….and Joy…
Patient and kind,
Do not fear,
Grace is for you,
And, I'll give you life eternally.

On the twelfth day of Christmas, Jesus said to me:
Speak words of goodness,
Be a cheerful giver,
Share love with others,
Make choices wisely,
You're now forgiven,
Love's always with you,
Honor your parents,
Love…Peace….and Joy…
Patient and kind,
Do not fear,
Grace is for you,

(everyone together)
And I'll give you life eternally.

Hi. My Name is Alice.

by Paul Shepherd

SUMMARY: *A young girl celebrates the cycle of life and the reason for the season.*

CHARACTERS:
Young Alice: eight-year-old girl
Teenage Alice: teen girl
Young Adult Alice: young adult woman
Young Adult John: young adult man
Middle-Age Alice: middle-aged woman
Middle-Age John: middle-aged man
Jacob: nineteen-year-old boy
Christopher: fifteen-year-old boy
Senior Alice: older woman

SETTING: *none*

PROPS: *baby doll wrapped in blanket*

COSTUMES: *regular everyday clothes*

Characters will walk to the middle of the stage then exit after each speaks.

Young Alice enters.

YOUNG ALICE: Hi. My name is Alice. I love Christmas because it's so much fun. I get lots of things; some I expect and some I don't. My friends all talk about their special gifts and what they do with their families. Our church helps people who don't have gifts for their kids, and we collect food for the needy. I cry sometimes because I have so much, and they have so little. I wish Christmas were all year long. I just became a new believer so I know the real meaning and celebration of Christmas is about Jesus.

Exit stage.

Teenage Alice enters.

TEENAGE ALICE: Hi. My name is Alice. This is my favorite time of year. I love parties with friends and giving surprise gifts to all of them. This year I'm getting a new Mac and an iPhone. I need ... haha ... all the new gadgets to keep up with everything. My family is always together at Christmas, and I have happy memories of everyone's smiling faces. Some of my friends have parents who are separated or divorced, and I feel sad for them at Christmas. It should be such a happy time. I know the reason for Christmas is the celebration of Jesus and his birth.

Exit stage.

Young Adult Alice enters with Young Adult John, who is holding the baby doll..

YOUNG ADULT ALICE: Hi. My name is Alice. This is John, my husband. We're celebrating five years of marriage and the birth of our first son, Jacob. This season has a special meaning as we celebrate Jacob's first Christmas and the birth of our Savior, Jesus Christ. I've saved an ornament for Jesus on each of my Christmas trees, so we will start a new tradition for Jacob with a new ornament for him as well. Jesus is the reason.

All exit stage.

Middle-Age Alice enters with Middle-Age John, Jacob, and Christopher.

MIDDLE-AGE ALICE: Hi. My name is Alice. You remember John and Jacob? This is our youngest son, Christopher. He was born on Christmas Day and now has fifteen ornaments to celebrate his birthdays. Jacob has nineteen. While we create Christmas ornaments and give gifts each year, we celebrate Jesus and His birth. We celebrate Him all year long, but especially at this time.

All exit stage.

Senior Alice enters.

SENIOR ALICE: Hi. My name is Alice. I lost John last year, and this will be my first Christmas in forty-five years without him. Both my sons are married and have children, so this Christmas will be a new beginning for all of us. No longer will John be here. Throughout the many celebrations, John and I always tried to keep life and family in perspective. Jesus was born to bring hope and new life to all mankind, and then he went to heaven to prepare a place for us. The cycle of life moves on, but Jesus' love is always there. Celebrate him.

Exit stage.

What Do You Want For Christmas?

by Paul Shepherd

SUMMARY: *Two men reminisce about memories and loss at Christmas while granddaughters are thinking of ways to make this Christmas special.*

CHARACTERS:
Two men with white hair.
Two teenage girls

SETTING: *the two older men sit on chairs on one side of the stage; the two girls stand on the opposite side*

PROPS: *two chairs, one small wrapped gift box*

COSTUMES: *regular clothes*

Spotlight on the men.

MAN 1: December again. Seems like it was just yesterday and it was last Christmas and here I am … here we are. I think we talked about this last year, how quickly time moves along, as you get older.

MAN 2: I know. Losing Sally last year was really hard and this is the first Christmas without her. Fifty years together and some wonderful things to remind me of her. Makes me smile when I recall all the good times with the family around during the holidays.

MAN 1: You guys were perfect together. I know the time is coming when June or I will be leaving, and it's times like Christmas that marks the end of another year. Or, the beginning. I know you'll be with your family, but please know you can spend time with us as well.

MAN 2: Sally loved you and June. The boys will be coming up, and we'll make plans to spend time with you. At least watch a ball game or something.

Spotlight moves to the girls.

GIRL 1: I love Christmas. Gifts. Food. Clothes. Stuff. I love the songs. I love the decorations. I love the cheer and how everyone seems happy. I just love, love it!

GIRL 2: Me too. I will miss my grandmother this year. I can't believe she's gone and won't be with us this year. My granddad misses her so much. You know, they were married fifty years. I can't imagine fifty years with any boy I've ever met. How about you?

GIRL 1: Ha. Maybe Dan. He seems like a good guy. Loves his Mom. Goes to church. And, he has blue eyes. Ha!

GIRL 2: You and those blue eyes. My grandmother had the prettiest blue eyes, and when she smiled, she could light up the room.

GIRL 1: I remember. She was always so kind to me. She taught me in Bible study and made me think about what's been important in life. I love stuff, but stuff is so temporary ... you know?

GIRL 2: I've heard that over and over from her. I hope someday to find a man like my granddad who has been as committed to God and the church as they have been.

Spotlight moves to the men.

MAN 2: I remember our first Christmas in Texas. We lived in a little apartment with no kitchen table or chairs. That Sally … she decorated that apartment with handmade ornaments and garland … almost like Macy's. We had a little skinny tree I found along the road, and she turned that tree into a glowing wonder. Her touch on my life, and the lives of others, was really an extension of her love of Jesus.

MAN 1: *(smiling)* She touched all our lives, and I always felt I'd been to church after spending time around her.

MAN 2: As much as I will miss her, the family will be lost without her. She loved to give gifts to all the family. Each one was a special purchase. She told little stories about each gift so the recipients felt they were the only person in the world. Kind of like Jesus' love for us.

MAN 1: Last year she gave June a bracelet she'd made. She said, "Each stitch was a loop of love, specially wound for you." June still wears that bracelet.

Spotlight moves to the girls.

GIRL 1: My family's going to Colorado to ski this Christmas. I love the snow in Aspen. What an awesome time to spend with family in the mountains. I love skiing. I love fireplaces.

GIRL 2: This year is going to be the first without my grandmother. We'd always go to her house. It's like being in wonderland with all the decorations. She always made one new decoration to add to all the years she and grand-dad were together. Then she gave each member of the family a special gift. They weren't expensive gifts, but something meaningful. Last year she made me a book-mark for my Bible. It was taken from a dress she wore at their twenty-fifth anniversary party. You've seen it. The top has a cross.

GIRL 1: That bookmark is so unique. I've always thought it was pretty.

GIRL 2: She did that for everyone. You couldn't help but smile and cry at the same time as she looked at you…and told her story. Reminds me of how Jesus must have looked at everyone.

GIRL 1: What are you going to do this year? She won't be there.

GIRL 2: I've been thinking about that. For fifteen years, every Christmas. I think I know what I can do.

Spotlight moves to the men.

MAN 2: The boys will be bringing their families again, and we'll figure out everything. They all have wonderful wives, and I have the best grandkids in the world. They never seem to mind coming over to see "old people." They even leave their phones and iPads at home.

MAN 1: They do? They must love you very much.

Lights up on the whole stage. The girls cross the stage to where the men are sitting.

GIRL 1: Hi there, you handsome men. You're looking great today!

GIRL 2: (*to Man 2*) Hi Granddad. Love that sweater you're wearing. I have something for you. Grandmother always gave me a special gift, and I have them all. It always made me feel loved and special. She always told me that Jesus had that special love for each of us and was the reason we came together each Christmas to celebrate his birth. I made this little gift for you … to let you know how much I love you and how special you are to me. You both have been so important to me, and I want this Christmas to be a time to celebrate Jesus and grandmother.

She hands the gift box to Man 2.

MAN 2: The greatest gift you can give me is to see the Christian lady you've become.

Who Is This Jesus?

by Paul Shepherd

SUMMARY: *The animals that surrounded baby Jesus on the night He was born talk about the events that led them all to that incredible night.*

CHARACTERS:
Joseph and Mary
Three people to play the sheep
Two people to play the cows
Three people to play the camels
One person to play the mouse
One person to play the donkey
One Angel

SETTING: *Christmas night*

PROPS: *simple stable and manger, chair for Mary to sit, baby doll wrapped in simple cloth*

COSTUMES: *Masks or robes for sheep, cows, camels, mouse, and donkey*

The cows stand inside the stable

COW 1: I love this stable. Good straw. Fresh air, most of the time. You can see the stars and moon.

COW 2: I like it here, too, but I hear we have visitors coming tonight.

COW 1: Really? Here? What kind of visitors?

COW 2: A man and a woman on a donkey. I heard they traveled all the way from Nazareth. And … she's having a baby. I heard them say they're putting the new baby in the trough where we eat.

COW 1: No way. Where are we going to eat? You know I like to eat.

COW 2: It'll be fine. You need to lose weight anyway.

COW 1: Why aren't they staying in the inn?

COW 2: No room in the inn.

The sheep stand in a group, outside and at a distance from the stable.

SHEEP 1: What's all the noise?

SHEEP 2: Bahhhh. Turn off the music and cut the lights. Who is doing all that singing?

SHEEP 3: Angels? ANGELS? Why are they singing? Bahhhh.

SHEEP 1: "Glory to God in the highest, and peace on earth to people who enjoy his favor!" What does that mean?

SHEEP 2: Can someone tell me what's going on?

SHEEP 1: Something about packing up and heading into town. The shepherds are waking all the sheep and packing their bags.

SHEEP 3: Okay … let's round everyone up and go to Bethlehem. Move it.

(Move to the stable and sit to one side.)

(The camels walk slowly toward the stable from the opposite side as the sheep.)

CAMEL 1: I don't know about you, but I thought we'd never get here. You know I can go months without water, but thank goodness they followed that star at night so we didn't have to walk so much during the day. It was really hot in the desert.

CAMEL 2: I know. So glad we finally got to Bethlehem so we can rest. Whew!

CAMEL 3: I kept hearing about why we were traveling all this way. Did you guys understand this talk about "a King"? Who is this King? Must be someone really important.

CAMEL 1: I was expecting some big palace, a good rubdown, and a bath after all this travel, but we're here ... at some stable. Are you kidding?

CAMEL 2: Right. Sheep? Cows? What's up with this?

CAMEL 3: Somehow I think we're here for something incredibly important.

(Arrive and stop next to the stable opposite the sheep.)

(The mouse stands in the middle of the stable.)

MOUSE: Everyone, listen up! This is my stable, and I know everything that goes on here. Cows, sit over there. Camels, in the back. Let's move it. Sheep, come up front. Please lay down here so everyone can see me. We're all here today to see something amazing! Something you never could have imagined. History! We're here to witness history that will change people's lives forever.

(The Angel, who has been standing in the rear, steps up to the

front of the stage.)

ANGEL: "Do not be afraid; for behold, I bring you good news of great joy which will be for all the people; for today in the city of David there has been born for you a Savior, who is Christ the Lord. 'This will be a sign for you: you will find a baby wrapped in cloths and lying in a manger.'"

Mary walks in carrying baby Jesus. Joseph follows her along with the donkey. Mary sits down and lays Jesus in the manger.

(The donkey stands beside Joseph.)

DONKEY: I was the one they chose. I carried Mary and the baby to Bethlehem. I'm tired, but I listened to them talk along the way and now I understand … it's all about the baby, Jesus. He is the Lord of all creation. Heaven's perfect lamb. The sleeping child you see here is the great, I AM.

All animals applaud.

Contributing Authors

DIANA C. DERRINGER

Diana C. Derringer is a writer and blogger. Her work appears in more than forty publications for children, youth, families, and seniors. These include *Clubhouse, Pockets, devozine, ENCOUNTER, Open Windows, The Upper Room, Country Extra, ParentLife, Missions Mosaic, The Christian Communicator,* and *Mature Living.* She also writes radio drama for Christ to the World Ministries. Devotions, drama, practical living, lessons from life, poetry, planning guides, and more find a home in her portfolio. She belongs to the American Christian Writers and the Kentucky State Poetry Society. Visit her at www.dianaderringer. com.

PAUL SHEPHERD

Paul Shepherd has worked in Christian publishing for over 40 years. The early years in publishing were spent with Thomas Nelson, primarily in field and national account sales. In the late 1980s, he became VP Sales and Marketing for Riverside Distributors and World Bible Publishers. In the 1990s, he worked with major New York publishers including Random House and Warner Books. In early 2000s, he became Acquisitions Editor for Elm Hill Books, a division of J. Countryman and Thomas Nelson. During those years, he acquired and developed several authors in Christian publishing. Currently, he is developing authors as a consultant and literary agent while continuing to write small inspirational stories for publication.

Ten Questions for Planning Your Best Christmas Programs

1. Who is the audience?

2. How can you approach this Christmas in a fresh way?

3. Will you need special features including video, dance, music, and staging?

4. Will you want the audience to participate?

5. How long is the service?

6. Will you do one service for kids, youth, and adults?

7. Have times been set for services?

8. Will you need extra seating during the service?

9. What is your budget?

10. Do you need extra volunteers?

Church Survey

Thank you for using this Christmas program book. We would like to know what you think of the dramas. Please send us an email with your comments and your thoughts on how we might serve you better.

Paul Shepherd, Shepherd Publishing Services
jjppss@reagan.com

1. What did you think of the program book?

   Excellent   Average   Below Average

2. Which of the following would you like to see more of in future books?

   Dramas   Poems   Stories   Songs

3. Please tell us why you bought the book:

4. What other improvements would you like to see?

5. Would you use an Easter program book?

6. Would you use a year-round program book?

7. Which program book did you use?

   Kids   Youth   Adults

8. If you know of an author who would be interested in contributing to our books, please provide us their name and contact information:

9. Please share the name of your church, primary contact name, phone number, and email address:

Program Planning

_____

_____

_____

_____

_____

_____

_____

_____

_____

_____

_____

_____

_____

_____

_____

_____

_____

_____

_____

_____

_____

_____

_____

Program Planning

_____

_____

_____

_____

_____

_____

_____

_____

_____

_____

_____

_____

_____

_____

_____

_____

_____

_____

_____

_____

_____

_____

Program Planning

Program Planning

Program Planning

_____

_____

_____

_____

_____

_____

_____

_____

_____

_____

_____

_____

_____

_____

_____

_____

_____

_____

_____

_____

_____

_____

Program Planning

_____

_____

_____

_____

_____

_____

_____

_____

_____

_____

_____

_____

_____

_____

_____

_____

_____

_____

_____

_____

_____

Printed in the USA
CPSIA information can be obtained
at www.ICGtesting.com
JSHW012043140824
68134JS00033B/3235